SONNY ROLLINS

CONTENTS

Foreword

In recent years, with proliferation of transcribed solos and the growing awareness of their value as teaching tools, it has become apparent to many jazz educators that simply memorizing a solo and playing it is not maximizing the potential of the technique as a learning experience. By the inclusion of in depth analysis, selected discography and bibliography, biographical data, a list of innovations, a genealogy, etc., as well as actual transcriptions of important solos, these books represent an attempt to place the study of recorded solos in a more meaningful context.

In many respects the jazz improvisor is a composer and as such might profit from being exposed to the same regimen and disciplines as a composer *per se*. One such discipline has to do with learning to write or play by imitating various models. Virtually every composer has gone through the stage of writing pieces in the style of Bach, Bartok, Stravinsky, Ellington and others. In imitating a particular composer the neophyte must learn and assimilate the harmonic, melodic, and rhythmic language of that composer. He must be able to project in a reasonably accurate fashion what that composer will do, given a particular set of musical options. This type of learning experience becomes doubly important when the composer under scrutiny is one of the giants who in one area or another is responsible for transforming the aesthetic. For instance, in any given period a handful of innovators is responsible for introducing new concepts into the music or simply reinterpreting or reshaping the extant language consistent with imperatives of that time.

It seems to this writer that the jazz player might profitably adapt an approach similar to that of the budding composer in learning his craft. With that end in mind this series of style studies has been designed to provide a modus operandi for studying, analyzing, imitating and assimilating the idiosyncratic and general facets of the styles of various jazz giants throughout the history of the music.

Although a model styles and analysis work sheet is provided, the reader may want to modify it or design another one which fits his or her specific needs. In any event, the aspiring jazz player is encouraged to completely dissect the improvisations as well as the tunes on which they are based. (This is absolutely mandatory in the case of bebop tunes whose patterns, melodic lines and harmonic structures comprise a substantial portion of the vocabulary of every contemporary jazz musician).

Relationship Of Chords To Scales

Major Family

Chord Type (I)	Scale Form
Major — 1 3 5 7 9	Major 1 2 3 4 5 6 7 8
Major (♯4) 1 3 5 7 9 ♯11	Lydian 1 2 3 ♯4 5 6 7 8
Major (♯4 ♯5) 1 3 ♯5 7 9 ♯11	Lydian Augmented 1 2 3 ♯4 ♯5 6 7 8
Major (♭6 ♯9) 1 3 5 7 9 11 13	Augmented 1 ♯2 3 5 ♭6 7 1
Major 1 3 5 7 9	diminished 1 ♭2 ♭3 ♮3 ♯4 5 6 ♭7 8
Major 1 3 5 7 9	Harmonic Major 1 2 3 4 5 ♭6 7 8
Major 1 3 5 7 9	blues 1 ♭3 ♮3 4 ♯4 5 ♭7 8
Major 1 3 5 7 9	minor pentatonic 1 ♭3 4 5 ♭7 8
Major 1 3 5 7 9	Major pentatonic 1 2 3 5 6 8
	Seventh scale (Major) 1 2 3 4 5 ♯5 6 7 8

minor Family

Chord Type	Scale Form
minor, tonic (I) Function	Dorian 1 2 ♭3 4 5 6 ♭7 8
	Natural minor 1 2 ♭3 4 5 ♭6 ♭7 8
	Phrygian 1 ♭2 ♭3 4 5 ♭6 ♭7 8
	Ascending Melodic minor 1 2 ♭3 4 5 6 7 8
	Harmonic minor 1 2 ♭3 4 5 ♭6 7 8
	minor pentatonic 1 ♭3 4 5 ♭7 8
	Blues 1 ♭3 4 ♯4 5 ♭7 8
minor 7th (II) Function	Dorian 1 2 ♭3 4 5 6 ♭7 9
	Ascending melodic minor 1 2 ♭3 4 5 6 7 8
	Harmonic minor 1 2 ♭3 4 5 ♭6 7 1
	minor Pentatonic 1 ♭3 4 5 ♭7 8
	Blues 1 ♭3 4 ♯4 5 7 8
	diminished (start with whole step) 1 2 ♭3 4 ♯4 ♯5 6 7 8
	Seventh scale (start on the 4th) 1 2 3 4 5 6 ♭7 ♮7 8

Dominant Family

Chord Type	Scale Form
Dominant 7th unaltered 1 3 5 ♭7 9	Mixolydian 1 2 3 4 5 6 ♭7 8
	Lydian Dominant 1 2 3 ♯4 5 6 ♭7 8
	Major Pentatonic 1 2 3 5 6 8
	minor Pentatonic 1 ♭3 4 5 ♭7 8
	Blues 1 ♭3 ♮3 4 ♯4 5 ♭7 8
	Seventh scale 1 2 3 4 5 6 ♭7 ♮7 1
Dominant 7th ♯11 1 3 5 ♭7 9 ♯11	Lydian dominant 1 2 3 ♯4 5 6 ♭7 8
Dominant 7th ♭5, ♯5 or both 1 3 ♭5 ♭7 1 3 ♯5 ♭7 1 3 (♭5 ♯5) ♭7	Whole Tone 1 2 3 ♯4 ♯5 ♯6

Chord Type	Scale Form
Dominant 7th (♭9)	Diminished
1 3 5 ♭7 ♭9	1 ♭2 ♭3 ♮3 #4 5 6 ♭7 8
Dominant 7th #9	Diminished 1 ♭2 ♭3 ♮3 #4 5 ♭7 8
1 3 5 ♭7 #9	Diminished whole tone
	1 ♭2 ♭3 ♮3 #4 #5 #6 8
	Dorian 1 2 ♭3 4 5 6 ♭7 8
	Blues 1 ♭3 ♮3 4 #4 5 ♭7 8
	minor pentatonic 1 ♭3 4 5 ♭7 8
Dominant 7th ♭9 and #9	diminished 1 ♭2 ♭3 ♮3#4 5 6 ♭7 8
	diminished whole tone
	1 ♭2 ♭3 ♮3 #4 #5 #6 8
	minor pentatonic 1 ♭3 4 5 ♭7 8
	Blues 1 ♭3 ♮3 4 #4 5 ♭7 8
Dominant 7th ♭5 and ♭9	diminished
	1 ♭2 ♭3 ♮3 #4 5 6 ♭7 8
	diminished whole tone
	1 ♭2 ♭3 ♮3 #4 #5 #6 8
	minor pentatonic 1 ♭3 4 5 ♭7 8
	Blues 1 ♭3 ♮3 4 #4 5 ♭7 8
Dominant 7th	diminished scale
♭5 and ♭9 13 ♭5 ♭7 ♭9	1 ♭2 ♭3 ♮3 #4 5 6 ♭7 8
#5 and #9 13 #5 ♭7 #9	minor pentatonic
♭5 and #9 13 ♭5 ♭7 #9	1 ♭3 4 5 ♭7 8
#5 and ♭9 13 #5 ♭7 ♭9	Blues 1 ♭3 ♮3 4 #4 5 ♭7 8
(and / combination)	

Half-diminished chords

Chord Type	Scale Form
(half-diminished 7th	Locrian 1 ♭2 ♭3 4 ♭5 ♭6 ♭7 8
(∅7)	Locrian #2 — 1 2 ♭3 4 ♭5 ♭6 ♭7 8
or	Seventh scale (start on ♭6)
	1 2 3 4 5 6 ♭7 ♮7 1
minor 7th (♭5)	diminished (start with whole step)
1 ♭3 ♭5 ♭7	1 2 ♭3 4 #4 #5 6 7 8
	blues 1 ♭3 4 #4 5 ♭7 8

diminished chords

diminished 7th	diminished scale
(o7)	(start with whole step)
1 ♭3 ♭5 6	1 2 ♭3 4 #4 #5 6 7 8

Because the scale(s) which I refer to as seventh scales have not been dealt with in any book except my Improvisational Patterns. The Bebop Era, Volumes 1, 2, and 3 (published by Charles Colin; 315 West 53rd Street; New York, N.Y. 10019), perhaps a word of explanation would be in order:

1. The scale usually moves in basic eighth note patterns.

2. The scale always starts on a downbeat and a chord tone.

3. More often than not, the scale is played in a descending fashion.

4. When playing a major scale over a I chord, an extra half step occurs between 5 and 6 if the scale starts on the root, 3rd, 5th, or 7th of the chord (1 7 6 $\flat$6 5 4 3 2 1).

5. When playing a mixolydian scale over a II, V7 or VII chord, an extra half step usually occurs between the tonic and the flat seventh of the scale, as in the following:

Dmi7, G7, B = G G$\flat$ F E D C B A G
　　　　　　　　 1 7 $\flat$7 6 5 4 3 2 1

This rule is operative as long as the scale starts on the root, 3rd, 5th, or 7th of the V7 chord.

Owing to the importance of the seventh scale and its pervasiveness in virtually every chord playing situation, I have chosen to place the scale in brackets whenever it appears in the analyses.

Transcribing Solos From Records

One of the undersirable consequences resulting from a surfeit of teaching methods, improvisation books, and other educational aids has been the virtual disappearance of the player who accelerates learning by playing along with records.

It is lamentable that we teachers, authors, educators, and performers from the period B.J.M.B. (before jazz method books) have forgotten that we learned our craft by playing along with and studying the solos of our jazz heroes.

While no rational educator would advocate a return to those times when recordings were the principal means of learning, it behooves us to re-examine the very important role that record transcriptions can and must play in the development and continued growth of jazz players.

For the young jazz player, listening to, analyzing, and playing along with records is an absolute must if he is to learn the language, its syntax, grammar inflections, etc. The situation for the young player is not unlike that of a student learning to speak a foreign language. While books, flash cards and other visual aids are invaluable, they can never supplant hearing and imitating the spoken word. Even our native language is learned best through imitation of those around us; father, mother, brother, sister, nurse, etc. A child growing up in a French-speaking environment does not, as a consequence, speak German; he speaks French. Unless the budding jazz player is in an aural environment where the language of jazz is spoken (played), he will not learn that language. Subtlety, correct use of inflection, a feeling for swing, interpretation, style, etc., are all things that are most effectively learned through the repeated hearing of those players who first defined the music.

For the advanced jazz player, listening, analyzing, and transcribing are equally valuable if growth is to be continuous. Although the ends may be different and actual transcription, either written or played, may not take place; every good jazz player has a mandate to listen in a disciplined fashion to the music of his contemporaries. How else to stay abreast of the myriad, sometimes violent, changes taking place in this continually evolving music?

Sometimes new techniques, different approaches, new harmonic, rhythmic, and melodic ideas are more easily grasped when repeated listening is possible, hence the value, again, of record transcription.

The following aids to transcribing are offered:

1. Check turntable for key (pitch). Use common sense or some other referential, such as a tune on the album where the key is known. Adjust speed of turntable to a desired pitch.

2. Record solo on 7½ ips on tape (two levels beneath) Try to record from at least one chorus before (safety with changes, tempo, feel, etc.).

3. Listen to entire solo for:
    a. length (number of choruses)
    b. general shape, feel, form, etc
    c. changes

4. If faster than moderate tempo, make initial transcription at half speed, 3¾ ips.
    a. If possible, transcribe one measure of phrase at a time
       Listen, sing, write.
    b. Play preceding phrase, then new phrase as before

If a rhythm or pitch is troublesome, try to solve it through repeated listening and isolation. If necessary, slow to 1½ ips and stop on the note or rhythm group.

If a double time persists, transcribe it as though in 4/4 time, i e

in finished form.

If a piece is particularly complex rhythmically, you might bar off the entire solo, transcribe the first beat in each measure, then beat 3, later filling in missing notes. Sometimes educated guesses might be made based on melodic or rhythmic practices *au courante* A certain degree of predictability usually exists to the attuned ear

5. Once the solo is complete, verify at half speed by playing along on your instrument. Add inflections, dynamics, accents, slurs, etc

6. Play at the actual tempo for missed notes, etc Verify at the actual tempo.

Sonny Rollins
A Selected Bibliography

Arrigoni, A. "Qualcosa sta cambiando." *Musica Jazz,* June 1960, pp. 17-21

Arvantis, G. and others. "A propos d'un comeback." (Recording) *Jazz Hot,* November 1962, p. 9.

Atkins. "Sonny in London." *Jazz Monthly,* March 1965, pp. 29-30.

Avakian, G. "Sonny Meets Hawk and How It Happened." *Jazz,* October 1963, p. 17.

Ayler, A. "Meme musique in Brazilian." *Jazz Hot,* April 1975, pp. 14-15.

Balliett, W. "Jazz Concerts." *New Yorker,* February 3, 1962, p. 98.

Balliett, W. "Jazz Records." *New Yorker,* June 15, 1957, p. 78.

Buday, D. "Caught in the Act." *down beat,* July 15, 1966, p. 31.

Burks. "Festival in Black." *Rolling Stone,* May 31, 1969, p. 24.

Carles. "Sonny est cher." *Jazz Magazine,* January 1967, pp. 12-13.

_____. "Caught in the Act." *Melody Maker,* December 1, 1973, p. 24.

Cerulli, D. "Theodore Walter Rollins." *down beat,* July 10, 1958, pp. 16-17.

_____. "Close Shave in Japan for Tenorist Rollins." *down beat,* April 18, 1968, p. 14.

Clouzet, J. and Delorme, M. "Trois aus de reflextion." *Jazz Magazine,* March 1963, pp. 32-34.

_____. "Coming Up for the Third Dynasty." *Melody Maker,* March 26, 1966, p. 8.

_____. "Concert Reviews." *Variety,* April 2, 1969, p. 63.

Coss, B. "Return of Sonny." *down beat,* June 4, 1962, pp. 13-14.

_____. "Le due Rollins, *Jazz Magazine,* January 1966, pp. 22-25.

_____. "Les dauphins." *Jazz Magazine,* October 1961, p. 29.

Dawbarn, B. "Tenor Enigma Heading Our Way." *Melody Maker,* January 2, 1965, p. 6.

Delmas. "Traditions & Contradictions." *Jazz Hot,* July-August 1974, pp. 14-17.

Delorme, M. "Sonny au Jazzland." *Jazz Hot,* January 1967, p. 9.

_____. "Disque du mois." *Jazz Magazine,* November 1972, p. 44.

Feather, L. "Blindfold Test." *down beat,* August 2, 1962 (Part I), p. 29, August 16, 1962 (Part II), p. 29.

Feather, L. "Rollins in 3/4 Time." *down beat,* December 12, 1957. p. 39.

Fiofori, T. "Le deuxieme retour de Rollins." *Jazz Magazine,* November 1971, pp. 10-15.

Fiofori, T. "Efterlaengtad erme-back." *Orkester Journalen,* November 1971, pp. 8-9.

Fiofori, T. "Re-entry: The New Orbit of Sonny." *down beat,* October 14, 1971, pp. 14-15.

Fiofori, T. "Sonny Shines Again." *Melody Maker*, July 24, 1971, p. 12.

____. "Five Guggenheims to Artists in Jazz Field." *down beat*, June 8, 1972, p. 9.

____. "Five-Spot NY." *Variety*, April 29, 1964, p. 81.

Fremer, B. "Recordings." *Orkester Journalen*, September 1957, pp. 12-13.

Fremer, B. "Sonny Rollins." *Orkester Journalen*, July-August 1957, pp. 12-13, October 1957, pp. 10-11.

Fremer, B. "Sonny Rollins." *Orkester Journalen*, March 1959, pp. 14-15.

Gallagher, J. "Caught in the Act." *down beat*, July 24, 1969, p. 26.

Gerber, A. "Rollins va du pont." *Jazz Magazine*, February 1969, pp. 34-96.

____. "Caught in the Act." *down beat*, July 24, 1969, p. 26.

Giddins. "Rollins Record Dates Spots Soprano Sax." *down beat*, October 12, 1972, p. 10.

Gitler, I. "Caught in the Act." *down beat*, October 3, 1968, p. 4.

Goldberg, I. "The Further Adventures of Sonny Rollins." *down beat*, August 26, 1965, pp. 19-21.

Grigson. "Directions in Modern Jazz." *Jazz Monthly*, September 1961, p. 16.

Guastone. "Ecco, colti dopo i concerti, i guidiyi di alcuin jazz now." *Musica Jazz*, February 1963, pp. 17-18.

Guastone. "Quattro chiacchiere con Giami Bassco su cinque sassofonisti." *Musica Jazz*, November 1960, p. 28.

Hadlock, D. "Caught in the Act." *down beat*, May 24, 1962, p. 41

Hadlock, D. "Freedom Suite." *Jazz Review*, May 1959, pp. 10-11.

Hadlock, D. "La Freedom Suite." *Jazz Hot*, July-August 1960, pp. 24-26.

Hadlock, D. "Sonny Rollins." *down beat*, December 11, 1958, p. 49.

Hansson. "Magnifik Rollins." *Orkester Journalen*, October 1968, p. 9.

Harrison, M. "Sonny Rollins." *Jazz Journal*, August 1960, pp. 7-8.

____. "Heard and Seen." *Coda*, August 1975, pp. 33-34.

Hentoff, N. "Sonny Rollins." *down beat*, November 28, 1956, pp. 15-16.

Houston, B. "_____." *Melody Maker*, April 22, 1967, p. 8.

Houston, B. "Caught in the Act." *Melody Maker*, April 1, 1967, p. 4.

Hultin, R. "Caught in the Act." *down beat*. September 16, 1971, pp. 37-38.

Hyder. "Rollins Sound Ideas." *Melody Maker*, August 3, 1974, p. 48.

____. "Incontro con Rollins." *Musica Jazz*, February 1963, pp. 6-7.

____. "In Person." *Jazz Monthly*, April 1962, pp. 25-26.

Ioakimidis. "Sonny Rollins et John Coltrane en parallele." *Jazz Hot*, September 1962, pp. 24-27; October 1962, pp. 22-25; and November 1962, pp. 22-24.

James. "Some Interesting Contemporaries." *Jazz & Blues*, January 1973, pp. 8-14.

James, M. "Sonny Rollins on Record 1949-1954." *Jazz Montly*, October 1959, pp. 7-11.

Priestly. "Second Opinion." *Melody Maker,* May 10, 1969, p. 8.

_____. "Record Review." *Coda,* 1972, No. 10, pp. 24-25.

_____. "Record Reviews: Next Album." *down beat,* November 9, 1972, p. 19.

_____. "Jazz Gallery NY." *Variety,* November 22, 1961, p. 16.

_____. "Jazz Records Nucleus." *Melody Maker,* January 17, 1976, p. 42.

Jepsen, J. "Sonny Rollins Diskografi." *Orkester Journalen,* September 1957, p. 54 and October 1957, p. 54.

Joans. "Musique noires en Hollande." *Jazz Magazine,* October-November 1973, pp. 34-35.

Jones. "A Personal Portrait of Sonny." *Melody Maker,* November 16, p. 12.

Kahn, H. "No Pianos for Me." *Melody Maker,* March 14, 1959, p. 5.

Koechlin, P. "Sonny." *Music (Chaix), February 1965, pp. 63-64.*

Kofsky. "Return of Sonny." Jazz Journal, May 1962, pp. 12-14.

Kopel, G. "Sonny Rollins." *Jazz Magazine,* January 1960, pp. 16-19.

Kopulos, G. "Need Now: Sonny Rollins." *down beat,* June 24, 1971, pp. 12-13.

Korall, B. "I've Talked Enough — Sonny—Trane & Ornette." *Melody Maker,* September 15, 1962, pp. 8-9.

Korall, B. "My Exile Has Paid Off." *Melody Maker,* December 23, 1961, p. 7.

Kotlowitz. "Sonny Rollins: the Gentle Blowhard." *Show,* April 1962, pp. 36-37.

Litweiler. "_____." *Jazz & Blues,* July 1973, pp. 12-13.

Locke. "On Stage." *Jazz & Blues,* June 1973, p. 14.

_____. "Manne-Hole LA." *Variety,* August 27, 1969, p. 58.

McRae. "AB Basics." *Jazz Journal,* March 1971, p. 14.

McRae. "A Tale of Two Sessions." *Jazz Journal,* July 1975, pp. 24-25.

McRae. "Jazz in Britain." *Jazz Journal,* May 1967, p. 10.

McRae. "Sonny." *Jazz Journal,* March 1965, pp. 6-7.

Mason and Others. "Interviews." *Jazz Magazine,* October-November 1973, pp. 34-35.

Millroth. "Moderna myter." *Orkester Journalen,* January 1975, pp. 8-9.

Morganstern, D. "Modern Reeds and How They Grew." *down beat,* May 14, 1959, p. 17.

Morgenstern. "Jazz Goes to Washington." *Musical America,* July 1962, pp. 18-19.

_____. "Les Nuits-Americaines." *Jazz Hot,* January 1974, p. 19.

Porter, B. "This Man Called Sonny." *down beat,* February 14, 1974, pp. 14-15.

_____. "Portrait." *Orkester Journalen,* March 1959, p. 50.

_____. "Portrait-Galleria." *Musica Jazz,* July-August 1962, p. 49.

_____. "Portrait-Galleria." *Musica Jazz,* March 1965, p. 48.

Postgate. "Between You and Me." *Jazz Monthly,* April 1960, p. 28.

Postif, F. "Au dela du bop." *Jazz Hot,* November 1966, pp. 27-28.

Priestly. "Max Roach and Sonny at Reading." *Jazz Monthly,* January 1967, pp. 11-12.

____. "Records: Sonny's Next Album." *Rolling Stone,* December 7, 1972, p. 66.

____. "Rollins au Gate." *Jazz Magazine,* November 1965, p. 19.

____. "Rollins Spannade." *Orkester Journalen,* February 1963, pp. 12-16.

____. "Rollins Tours Japan; Pianist Refused Entry." *down beat,* February 22, 1968, p. 10.

Rusel. "Sonny's Quartet at the Village Vanguard." *Jazz Digest,* June 1972, p. 10.

____. "Sabbatical." *New Yorker,* November 18, 1961, pp. 41-43.

Schonfield. "Musician." (Film Review.) *Jazz Journal,* January 1969, p. 8.

Schuller. "Sonny and the Challenge of Thematic Improvisation." *Jazz Review,* November 1958, pp. 6-9.

Scott. "Rollins: A Reminder of What It's All About." *Melody Maker,* January 16, 1965, p. 10.

____. "Seven Steps to Jazz." *Melody Maker,* May 14, 1966, p. 8.

____. "The Seville, H'wood." *Variety,* May 27, 1959, p. 69.

____. "Sonny." *Jazz Hot,* December 1974, p. 22.

____. "Sonny's Back." *down beat,* April 27, 1972, p. 9.

____. "Sonny's Back to Stay." *Melody Maker,* December 1, 1973, p. 24.

____. "Sonny in Japan." *Jazz & Pop,* April 1968, p. 8.

____. "Sonny Meets the Japanese Press." *down beat,* December 19, 1963, p. 16.

____. "Sonny Rollins chez RCA-Victor." *Jazz Magazine,* March 1962, p. 15.

____. "SPO Returns to Chicago." *down beat,* April 12, 1973, p. 12.

____. Talent in Action." *Billboard,* July 26, 1975, p. 41.

____. "The Verdict on Sonny Rollins." *Melody Maker,* February 13, 1965, p. 10.

____. "Village Gate NY." *Variety,* July 25, 1962, p. 98.

Wagner, J. "Seul contre tous." *Jazz Magazine,* March 1963, pp. 30-31.

West. "Return of a Recluse." *Jazz Forum,* October 1974, pp. 21-24.

Williams, M. "Caught in the Act." *down beat,* May 1, 1969, pp. 37-38.

Williams, M. "Extended Improvisation and Form: Some Solutions," *Jazz Review,* December 1958, pp. 13-15.

Williams, M. "_____." *Jazz Journal,* July 1966, pp. 24-26.

Williams, M. "The Novelist and the Hornman." *down beat,* September 5, 1968, p. 14.

Williams, M. "Some Achievements of a Decade Past." *Metro,* January 1961, p. 24.

Williams, M. "Tenor's Return." (Recording.) *Saturday Review,* June 16, 1962, pp. 36-37.

Wilson, J. "The Jazz Panorama." *Hifi Review,* April 1959, p. 80.

Wise. "Rollins is Still One of the Great Individualists." *Melody Maker,* December 10, 1966, p. 15.

Theodore Walter (Sonny) Rollins
Biographical Sketch

1929 September 7th, born in New York City.
Exposed to music very early in life.

1938 Studied piano very briefly at the urging of his mother.

1944 Started Alto Saxophone in High School.

1946 Changed to Tenor Saxophone.

1947 Began gigging around New York.

1949 First record date with Babs Gonzales.
Played with and hung around with Bud Powell, J.J. Johnson, Miles Davis, Fats Navarro, Charlie Parker, Thelonious Monk and others.

1949 Recorded with J.J., Bud and Miles.

1950 To Chicago with a group led by drummer Ike Day.
Soon returned to New York to freelance and ultimately spend six months with Miles Davis.

1953 Recorded with Miles and Bird.

1954 Back to Chicago to work at the *Beehive,* remained until 1955.
Joined the Max Roach, Clifford Brown Quartet replacing Tenor Saxophonist Harold Land. Had much contact with Charles Parker who befriended him and was a major influence on him.

1955 Performed and recorded with his own small groups including such sidemen as Kenny Dorham, Art Blakey, Ray Bryant, George Morrow, Donald Byrd, et al.

1956 Worked with Max and Clifford.

1957 Recorded *Tenor Madness* joined by Coltrane.
Left Max Roach.

1958 Reached a new level of popularity.
Much recording activity. (See discography).

1959 Went into voluntary exile during which time he practiced and studied.

1961 Returned to the music scene.

1962-63 Won *down beat* critics poll.

1963 Toured Japan and studied Zen Bhuddhism.

1965 To Europe playing in Berlin, London and the like.
Worked with various small groups.

1967-1970 Won *down beat* critics poll.

1969 Second tour of Japan and again went into retirement.

1971 He came back on the scene.

1972 Won a Guggenheim Fellowship.
Won *down beat* Readers Poll 1972-1975.

1973 Voted into the *down beat* Hall of Fame.

1974 Toured Europe.

Sonny Rollins Genealogy Chart

COLEMAN HAWKINS
LESTER YOUNG
BEN WEBSTER

ILLINOIS JACQUET
DON BYAS
DEXTER GORDON
LOUIS JORDAN
CHARLIE PARKER
THELONIOUS MONK
MILES DAVIS
LUCKY THOMPSON
LOCKJAW DAVIS
BUD POWELL

CLIFFORD BROWN

SONNY ROLLINS

JOHN COLTRANE

CANNONBALL ADDERLEY
SAM RIVERS
JOE HENDERSON
ARCHIE SHEPP
PAUL PLUMMER
JOHN GILMORE
JOE FARRELL

Sonny Rollins

PREFERRED TUNE TYPES

Standards including pop tunes, tin pan alley tunes and show tunes (often obscure). *Green Dolphin Street, The Surrey With The Fringe On Top, With A Song In My Heart, The Way You Look Tonight, Body And Soul, Wagon Wheels, Toot Toot Tootsie Goodbye*, etc.

Blues — usually *not* modified through substitution, addition of bridges, extended form, use of pedal points, etc. *Veird Blues, Blue Seven, Now's The Time*, etc.

Jazz Originals — his own and those of his contemporaries. *Well You Needn't, Bemsha Swing, Oleo, Doxy, Woody'n You, Tune Up*, etc.

Calypso Tunes — particularly his own originals. *St. Thomas* and *The Everywhere Calypso*.

Ballads — conventional tunes such as *Time On My Hands, A House Is Not A Home, Body And Soul*, off beat tunes such as *To A Wild Rose*, and jazz ballads such as *Round Midnight*.

PREFERRED TEMPOS

Sonny runs the gamut from non-tempoed unaccompanied cadenza like explorations to the fastest tempos imaginable. The greater body of his output falls in the moderate to fast range.

RHYTHMIC CHARACTERISTICS

1. Sonny has an uncanny metronomic sense. (The ability to maintain the form and placement within the time while consciously distorting the tempo and contracting and stretching the figures).

2. He makes extensive use of both double time, which he is able to execute at supersonic speeds, and half time or slowing down the time. The double time is usually sporadic. The slowing down is usually done through augmentation (stating the melodic materials in larger note values while maintaining the ratio, i.e., becomes).

3. Sonny very often uses rhythm for its own sake. He will sometimes improvise on a rhythmic pattern instead of on the melody or changes.

4. He has shown a decided penchant for tunes in 3/4 time such as *Valse Hot*.

5. He uses a large variety of rhythms even at faster tempos. This fact is made even more apparent because of his wide repertory of articulations.

6. Sonny, as a matter of course, will destroy the barline by stretching his melodies across sections of a tune. Very often he employs this technique to heighten the interest in the theme statement.

7. In Latin oriented tunes he leans toward extremely simple and repetitive rhythms preferring to maintain interest through melodic variations such as embellishment, trills, ornaments, etc.

8. His playing, particularly rhythmically, is greatly affected by his environment.

9. His playing is both reiterative and non-reiterative according to the musical circumstances.

10. Assymetrical rhythmic groupings are more likely to occur on ballads and in out of tempo sections of a tune.

11. He shows a preference for 4/4 and 3/4 time.

12. He swings at *all* tempos.

PREFERRED KEYS
Bb, F, C and Eb Major.
C and F minor.

SCALE PREFERENCES
Major and derivatives, whole tone, blues and pentatonic (particularly the major pentatonic), diminished, diminished/whole tone and the Lydian dominant.

The whole tone scale is very important particularly in early Sonny Rollins solos. From 1972 onward he shows a decided preference for both the major and minor pentatonic scales. The seventh scale is pervasive in his playing.

MELODIC CHARACTERISTICS
1. He uses fragmentation extensively as a technique for developing a melody.

2. He has a penchant for triadic material (i.e., *Doxy, St. Thomas, Airegin, Oleo, No Moe,* etc.)

3. His choice of melodic materials often seems a kind of stream of consciousness.

4. Ornamentation and embellishment are devices central to Sonnys melodic development or technique. (How they are used varies according to the musical context (i.e., in ballads and calypso tunes the ornamentation is often excessively florid, in other tunes the ornamentation is only slightly more than any other post bebop player).

5. His basic material is often quite simple and sometimes borders on being 'cute'.

6. In most instances the melodic material is quite heavily inflected particularly in blues and funk tunes.

7. Melodic contours are extremely varied with careful attention to the resultant shapes.

8. He almost always exercises great economy in his use of the basic material.

9. He makes use of a quasi-Prokofieff technique of resolving melodies to virtually any key however remote.

10. He makes use of the entire range of the instrument. His bottom range is exceptionally effective.

11. He has perhaps the most widely varied articulation of any jazz player.

12. His phrasing is usually regular and he almost always articulates cadence points to help delineate the form.

13. Tone and vibrato vary greatly according to the musical situation.

14. His technique of reducing melodic materials to the essential notes particularly in the head statement is in stark contrast to the ornamented and embellished outpourings of a developmental section.

15. Among other favorite devices are augmentation and diminution.

16. His melodic lines are often quite angular and often make much use of leading tones. When it's deemed appropriate he is a marvelously lyrical player.

17. 'Quotes' are central to Sonnys' melodic concept. The quotes are drawn from virtually every imaginable source. It is perhaps his fantastic memory that allows him to recall every melody with which he has come into contact. Among his favorite quotes are: *Camptown Races*, *The King And I*, Bebop tunes, patriotic and obscure tinpan alley songs.

18. He seems to have a real obsession with out of the way compositions such as: *I'm An Old Cowhand*, *Toot-Toot Tootsie*, *Wagon Wheels*, *Slow Boat To China*, etc.

HARMONIC CHARACTERISTICS

1. He makes much use of traditional minor third and tri-tone substitutions such as:
$$Dmi7 = \begin{matrix} Bmi7 \\ Abmi7. \\ Fmi7 \end{matrix}$$

2. He has a penchant for half step substitutions or side slips.

i.e., Dmi7 | G7 | C $\overset{Db}{|}$ C ||

3. He likes triadic structures.

4. He often chooses to play over a pedal point because of the freedom it affords.

5. The lack of piano on many tunes indicates Sonnys great comfort and ease with changes and form.

6. Very often his playing tends to be non-reiterative of the basic changes.

7. He often seems to use random substitutions.

8. He often creates his own highly individual harmonies with his lines.

9. He makes much use of chromatic passing chords.

10. He seems to prefer vertical tunes particularly those which provide a great challenge.

11. His favorite technique for creating tension is to deny a high predictability tune its resolution.

12. One of his favorite progressions or formulae is
III VI II V I, i.e., (Emi7 A7 Dmi7 G7 C C).

13. Like most other bebop players Sonny uses cycles most inventively.

PERFORMANCE PRACTICE

1. Most often Sonny prefers a thematic approach. Often the theme is the original melody but sometimes it is simply a melodic motive of his own design and choosing.

His methods for developing the chosen material are extremely varied and often unpredictable. The approaches include:

a. Transformation of the material through various techniques.
b. Sequence
c. Repetition
d. Transposition
e. Motivic development often through permutation.
f. Varying contour, texture.
g. Rhythmic unity and contrast.
h. Zeroing in on a single facet of the theme such as rhythm, shape, character, etc.
i. Fragmentation.
j. Sideslipping.

2. He often uses a cyclic approach. (Here again his remarkable memory retrieval system serves him well). Often a single idea serves as the point of reference.

3. His use of dynamics is exemplary.

4. As with Coltrane, Sonny is essentially a 'problem solving' player.

5. Quotes and use of other pre-extant materials often figure very prominently in his solos.

6. His solos often peak in exchanges with the drums or another horn player.

7. As with most other contemporary players quartal harmonies and pentatonic structures appear with increasing frequency in his recent playing.

8. Owing to his marvelous mind and prodigious technique Sonnys' playing always seems effortless.

Sonny Rollins The Composer

As with many other jazz musicians, Sonny Rollins' compositions are in many respects crystalization and codification of his improvisational beliefs. Studying his compositions can provide us with valuable insights into the workings of his improvisational mind. The following materials purport to generalize about some of the essentials in Rollins' compositional style.

Most of Sonny's tunes, regardless of category, share a readily identifiable tunefulness and attractiveness. Almost all are characterized by a deceptive simplicity and by extreme economy of material. As with Sonny's improvisations the themes are developed in a most logical fashion and with unpredictable wry twists — more often than not the main thematic material is either triadic or scalar. Sequence is perhaps the main technique usually used in the themes evolution. (For a discussion of Sonny's compositional techniques as well as musical philosophy read Chuck Bergs excellent interview with Rollins entitled *The Way Newk Feels*, **down beat** magazine April 7, 1977). Almost all of his themes share a riff like quality, particularly the *Calypso, Blues, Groove* and *Funk* type tunes.

Except for the *Blues* and *I Got Rhythm* type tunes, his compositions are rarely based on other compositions. His tunes are rarely as vertically complex as many of John Coltrane's. Throughout his career he has demonstrated a penchant for folk like material, such as that used in *Doxy, Keep Hold Of Yourself, St. Thomas* and *The Freedom Suite.*

As with his improvisations, the later years bring more and more excursions into modality and quartal areas of composition. Also, as with his improvisations, his writing is heavily indebted to the language constructs of the bebop era.

More specifically: The *Calypso tunes* are usually short, regular, utilize I, IV and V chords and in general exhibit an air of authenticity.

The *Blues and Groove tunes* more often than not draw on the blues and pentatonic scales, are riff oriented and basically triadic in structure. Most are in moderate tempos and are in F, Bb, Eb or Ab major or one of the more used minor keys.

The *bebop tunes* are in the mold of Charlie Parker's compositions but with Sonny's indelible imprint.

The *modal, pentatonic, funk* type tunes are usually extremely simple, make use of some sort of a bass ostinato and a rhythm and blues or rock beat. They too are usually based on blues and pentatonic scales and simple repetitive harmonies and rhythms.

The remainder of his output defies categorization. Often the forms are unusual, the phrase lengths unpredictable, and the overall effect quite refreshing.

TYPES

1. **Calypso Tunes**
   St. Thomas, Everywhere Calypso.

2. **Blues**
   Blues For Philly Joe, Blue Seven, Sonny Moon For Two, Solid, Tenor Madness.

3. **Groove Tunes**
   Doxy, Wail March, No Moe, Newk's Fadeaway, Swinging For Bumsy, Scoops.

4. **Bebop Type Tunes**
   Oleo, Airegin, Audubon, Pent-Up House, Valse Hot, The Stopper.

5. **Modal, Pentatonic, Funk**
   Notes' For Eddie, Playin' In The Yard, Keep Hold Of Yourself, The Cutting Edge, First Moves.

6. **Other**
   Decision, The Freedom Suite, East Broadway Rundown, The Bridge, John S.

Selected List of
Sonny Rollins Compositions

Airegin

Alfie's Theme

Alfie's Theme Differently

Audubon

Blessing In Disguise

Blue Seven

Blues For Philly Joe

Bluesnote

The Bridge

Brownskin Girl

Come, Gone

Cutie

The Cutting Edge

Decision

Doxy

East Broadway Run Down

The Everywhere Calypso

First Moves

The Freedom Suite

Funky Hotel Blues

Goof Square

He's Younger Then You Are

Hilo

John S.

Keep Hold Of Yourself

Kids Know

Love Man

Mambo Bounce

Moving Out

Newk's Fadeaway

No Moe

Notes For Eddie

Oleo

On Impulse

Paul's Pal

Pent-Up House

Pictures In The Reflection Of A Golden Horn

Plain Jane

Playin' In The Yard

St. Thomas

Scoops

Silk 'N' Satin

Solid

Sonny Moon For Two

The Stopper

Street Runner With Child

Strivers Row

Strode Rode

Swinging For Bumsy

Tenor Madness

Transition Theme For Minor Blues Or
   Little Malcolm Loves His Dad

Valse Hot

Wail March

Way Out West

Why Don't I

SONNY ROLLINS
A Discography of LP Recordings

Album Title	Label and No.
Babs Gonzales And His Orchestra	Capitol 57-60000, 57-60012
Strictly Bebop	Reissued on Capitol Jazz Classics, Vol. 13, M-11059
Early Bones	Prestige 24067 (Reissue)
with Bud Powell	Blue Note 1531, 1567, 1532, 1568, 1504
Miles Davis, Dig	Prestige 24054
First Recordings (with MJQ and others)	Prestige 7856E
also called	
Sonny Rollins And The Stars	Prestige 7269
Miles Davis Sextet	Prestige 734, 742, 140
with Miles Davis, (Jackie McLean)	Prestige
Miles And Horns	Prestige LP 7025
Sonny Rollins plus 4	Prestige LP 7039
Miles Davis And His Orchestra	Prestige 7044
Bag's Groove	Prestige 7109
Oleo	Prestige 7847
Jazz Classics	Prestige S-7433E
Worktime	Prestige S-7750E
3 Giants	Prestige S-7821E
Tenor Madness	Prestige 7047
Saxophone Colossus	Prestige S-7326E
Sonny Rollins	Prestige 24004
Saxophone Colossus And More	Prestige 24050E
Rollins Plays For Bird	Prestige 7553
Clifford Brown and Max Roach At Basin Street	EmArcy MG36070
	Reissued on TRIP TLP 5511
with Max Roach	EmArcy MG36098, Trp 5522 (Reissue)
Sonny Rollins	Blue Note 81542
Sonny Rollins	Blue Note LA-401-H2 (Reissue)
Way Out West	Contemporary 7530
Sonny Rollins	Blue Note 1558
Jazz Contrasts	Riverside 12-239
also	
But Beautiful	Milestone M47036
Freedom Suite	Riverside RS3010 also RLP 12-258

Freedom Suite Plus . . . . Milestone 47007
Night At The Village Vanguard . . . . Blue Note 81581
More From The Village Vanguard . . . . Blue Note LA 475-H2 (Reissue)
Sonny Rollins. . . . . Everest Archives 220E
Sonny Rollins And The Big Brass . . . . MGM C-776, 1002 also Verve V6-8430
Modern Jazz Quartet At Music Inn . . . . Atc. 1299
Newk's Time . . . . Blue Note 84001
Sonny Rollins And The Contemporary Leaders . . . . Contemporary 7564
The Genius Of Thelonious Monk . . . . Prestige 7656
The Bridge . . . . RCA APL 1-0859, also LSP-2527
On Impulse . . . . Impulse 91
East Broadway Rundown . . . . Impulse 9121
Alfie . . . . Impulse 9111
Reevaluations: Impulse Years . . . . Impulse 9236-2 (Reissue)
Next Album. . . . . Milestone 9042
Horn Culture. . . . . Milestone 9051
The Cutting Edge . . . . Milestone 9059

ADDITIONAL LISTINGS

Nucleus. . . . . Milestone 9064
The Way I Feel . . . . Milestone 9074
Dizzy Gillespie. . . . . Verve 2-2505
Energy Essentials . . . . Impulse D-9228
Decade Of Jazz, Vol. 2 . . . . Blue Note LA 159-62
Prestige Two-Fer Giants, Vol. 1. . . . . Prestige PRP-1
3 Giants . . . . Trip TRP X-5038
25 Years Of Prestige . . . . Prestige PRS-24046
The Sound Of Sonny . . . . Riverside SMJ-6139
Sonny Boy . . . . Xtra E5022, also on Prestige as Tour De Force, 7126
Mighty Monk . . . . Riverside RS3000
Now's The Time. . . . . RCA LSP 2927
Sonny Meets Hawk. . . . . RCA LPM 2712
Brilliant Corners: Thelonious Monk . . . . Riverside RLP 12-226
That's Him: Abbey Lincoln. . . . . Riverside RLP 12-251
Tenor Titan . . . . Verve 32
What's New . . . . RCA LPM 2572

ARTIST_____   Page_____

Title of composition:

Album:

Recording company:

Date:

Leader or sideman:

Instrument:

••

Tune type (circle one or more):	blues	jazz original
	ballad	bebop
	modal	Latin/Afro-Cuban/etc.
	standard	other (specify)_____
	free	

Tempo:

Key:

Dramatic devices (circle and describe):	vibrato
	slurs
	rips
	growls
	glissandi
	articulation (specify):
	alternate fingerings
	harmonics
	other (specify):

Tessitura:

Scale preferences (circle one or more):	major (and derivatives)	blues
	whole tone	pentatonic
	diminished	chromatic
	diminished whole tone	other (specify):
	lydian dominant	_____

Prevailing scale patterns:

Recurrent patterns: (A) II V7

  Turnbacks

  Cycles

  (B) Melodic patterns

  (C) Rhythmic patterns

  (D) Other formulae (I VI II V; III VI II V; half-step progressions, etc.)

••

PERFORMANCE PRACTICE

Developmental techniques: simple to complex
   (circle and describe)   complex to simple

                        single climax
                        many climaxes

                        vertical
                        horizontal

                        chord referential
                        thematic referential

                        use of sequence/call and response

                        use of quotes (what and where)

                        use of substitutions

                        rhythmic practices: double time
                                           half time
                                           assymetrical groupings
                                         reiterative
                                         non-reiterative
                      describe relationship to the basic time:

                      melody: folk-like   bluesy
                                  wide expressively   bebop
                                  narrow expressively   quartal
                                  riff-like   other (specify)_____

••

General Comments:

The musician should learn (memorize) the improvisation and play it with the record being careful to duplicate the time feel, inflections, vibrato, intensity, etc., as closely as possible. Next the player might take all of the II V7 patterns and transpose them to twelve keys varying tempo, volume, meter, register etc., until absolutely comfortable. Now the player might conceivably realize all of the II V7 situations in the tune being learned using one single pattern transposed to fit the harmonic situation. Next he should examine the various scale and melodic patterns to ascertain how the soloist uses them, then transpose the pattern to all keys, again varying musical components such as tempo, meter, volume, etc. Next he should do the same thing with cycles, turnarounds, etc., moving then from the highly specific environment of that particular composition to a more generalized musical situation.

ARTIST_____**Sonny Rollins**_____   Page_____

Title of composition: **Vierd Blues**

Album: **Oleo**

Recording company: **Prestige 7847**

Date: **June 6, 7847**

Leader or sideman: **Sideman**

Instrument: **Tenor Saxophone**

••

Tune type (circle one or more):   (blues)   (jazz original)
                                      ballad   (bebop)
                                      modal   Latin/Afro-Cuban/etc.
                                      standard   other (specify)_____
                                      free

Tempo: ♩=112

Key: **Concert B♭ (Tenor C)**

Dramatic devices (circle and describe):   (vibrato)
                                          (slurs)
                                          rips
                                          growls
                                          glissandi
                                          (articulation)(specify): **bebop phrasing**

                                          alternate fingerings
                                          harmonics
                                          other (specify):

Tessitura: **middle**

Scale preferences (circle one or more):   (major (and derivatives))   (blues)
                                          (whole tone)   pentatonic
                                          diminished   chromatic
                                          diminished whole tone   (other)(specify):
                                          lydian dominant   **seventh**

Prevailing scale patterns: **see attached sheets**

Recurrent patterns: (A) (II V7) **see attached sheets**

        Turnbacks

        Cycles

     (B) Melodic patterns **see attached sheets**

     (C) Rhythmic patterns

     (D) Other formulae (I VI II V; III VI II V; half-step progressions, etc.)

••

PERFORMANCE PRACTICE

Developmental techniques: simple to complex }
    (circle and describe)   complex to simple } **maintains same level**

                  single climax }
                  many climaxes } **maintains same level**

                  vertical
                  (horizontal)
                  (chord referential)
                  thematic referential

                  use of sequence/call and response

                  use of quotes (what and where)

                  use of substitutions

                  rhythmic practices: (double time)
                                    half time
                                    assymetrical groupings
                                  (reiterative)
                                  non-reiterative
                  describe relationship to the basic time: **on top**

                  melody: folk-like   (bluesy)
                          (wide expressively)   bebop
                          narrow expressively   quartal
                          riff-like   other (specify)_____

••

General Comments:

Vierd Blues

Sonny Rollins

Vierd Blues

Sonny Rollins

ARTIST_____ **Sonny Rollins**_____   Page_____

Title of composition: **Doxy**

Album: **Oleo**

Recording company: **Prestige 7847**

Date: **June 29, 1954**

Leader or sideman: **Sideman**

Instrument: **Tenor Saxophone**

....

Tune type (circle one or more):   blues   (jazz original)
                                         ballad   (bebop)
                                         modal   Latin/Afro-Cuban/etc.
                                         standard   other (specify)_____
                                         free

Tempo: ♩=128

Key: **Concert B♭ (Tenor C)**

Dramatic devices (circle and describe):   (vibrato)
                                          (slurs)
                                          rips
                                          growls
                                          glissandi
                                          (articulation) (specify): **varied**

                                          alternate fingerings
                                          harmonics
                                          other (specify):

Tessitura: **middle**

Scale preferences (circle one or more):   (major (and derivatives))   (blues)
                                          whole tone   pentatonic
                                          diminished   chromatic
                                          diminished whole tone   (other) (specify):
                                          lydian dominant   **seventh**

Prevailing scale patterns: **see attached sheets**

Recurrent patterns: (A) (II V7) **see attached sheets**

                    Turnbacks

                    Cycles

              (B) (Melodic patterns) **see attached sheets**

              (C) Rhythmic patterns

              (D) Other formulae (I VI II V; III VI II V; half-step progressions, etc.)

• •

PERFORMANCE PRACTICE

Developmental techniques: (simple to complex)
   (circle and describe)   complex to simple

                       (single climax)
                       many climaxes

                       (vertical)
                       (horizontal)

                       (chord referential)
                       thematic referential

                       (use of sequence) call and response

                       use of quotes (what and where)

                       use of substitutions

             rhythmic practices: (double time)
                       half time
                       assymetrical groupings
                       (reiterative)
                       non-reiterative
             describe relationship to the basic time: **on top**

             melody: folk-like   (bluesy)
                   (wide expressively)   (bebop)
                   narrow expressively   quartal
                   (riff-like)   other (specify)_____

• •

General Comments:

DOXY

6/29/54

DOXY

II V₇ Patterns

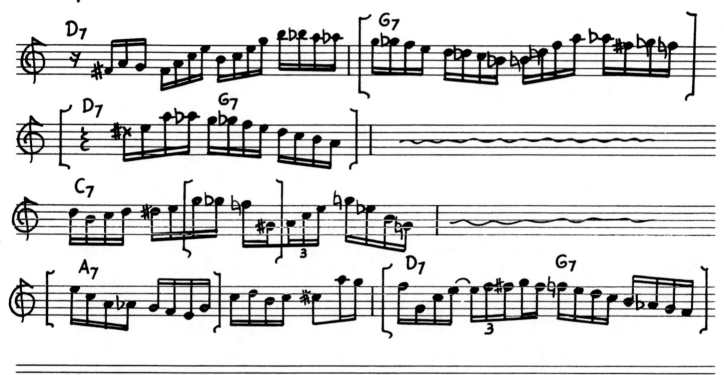

Melodic Patterns

ARTIST_____**Sonny Rollins**_____   Page_____

Title of composition: **Slow Boat to China**

Album: **Sonny Rollins and the Stars**

Recording company: **Prestige 7269**

Date: **December 1951**

Leader or sideman: **Leader**

Instrument: **Tenor Saxophone**

••

Tune type (circle one or more):

blues	jazz original
ballad	bebop
modal	Latin/Afro-Cuban/etc.
(standard)	other (specify)_____
free	

Tempo: ♩=112

Key: **Concert E♭ (Tenor F)**

Dramatic devices (circle and describe):

(vibrato)
(slurs)
rips
growls
glissandi
(articulation) (specify): **bebop phrasing**

alternate fingerings
harmonics
other (specify):

Tessitura: **middle**

Scale preferences (circle one or more):

(major (and derivatives))	blues
whole tone	pentatonic
diminished	chromatic
diminished whole tone	(other) (specify):
lydian dominant	**seventh**

Prevailing scale patterns: **see attached sheets**

Recurrent patterns: (A) II V7

           Turnbacks

                          see attached sheets

           Cycles

       (B) Melodic patterns

       (C) Rhythmic patterns

       (D) Other formulae (I VI II V; III VI II V; half-step progressions, etc.)

••

PERFORMANCE PRACTICE

Developmental techniques: simple to complex   **maintains same level**
   (circle and describe)   complex to simple

                       single climax   **maintains same level**
                       many climaxes

                       (vertical)
                       horizontal

                       (chord referential)
                       thematic referential

                       use of sequence/call and response

                       use of quotes (what and where)

                       use of substitutions

                       rhythmic practices: double time
                                          half time
                                          assymetrical groupings
                                        (reiterative)
                                        non-reiterative
                       describe relationship to the basic time: **on top**

                       melody: folk-like   bluesy
                              wide expressively   (bebop)
                            narrow expressively   quartal
                            riff-like   other (specify)_____

••

General Comments:

Slow Boat to China

Slow Boat to China

Sonny Rollins

ARTIST_____**Sonny Rollins**_____ Page_____

Title of composition: **Tenor Madness**

Album: **Tenor Madness**

Recording company: **Prestige LP 7047**

Date: **May 1956**

Leader or sideman: **Leader**

Instrument: **Tenor Saxophone**

••

Tune type (circle one or more):

(blues) (jazz original)
ballad (bebop)
modal Latin/Afro-Cuban/etc.
standard other (specify)_____
free

Tempo: ♩=176

Key: **B♭ concert (Tenor C)**

Dramatic devices (circle and describe):

(vibrato)
(slurs)
rips
growls
glissandi
(articulation) (specify): **varied**

alternate fingerings
harmonics
other (specify):

Tessitura: **middle to high**

Scale preferences (circle one or more):

(major (and derivatives)) (blues)
whole tone pentatonic
diminished chromatic
diminished whole tone (other) (specify):
lydian dominant _____**seventh**_____

Prevailing scale patterns: **see attached sheets**

Recurrent patterns: (A) II V7 **see attached sheets**

Turnbacks

Cycles

(B) Melodic patterns **see attached sheets**

(C) Rhythmic patterns

(D) Other formulae (I VI II V; III VI II V; half-step progressions, etc.)

••

PERFORMANCE PRACTICE

Developmental techniques: (simple to complex   **and back to simple**)
   (circle and describe)   complex to simple

single climax
(many climaxes)

(vertical)
(horizontal)

(chord referential) **but several references to the theme**
thematic referential

(use of sequence) call and response

use of quotes (what and where)

use of substitutions

rhythmic practices: (double time)
half time
(assymetrical groupings)
(reiterative)
non-reiterative
describe relationship to the basic time: **on top**

melody: folk-like   (bluesy)
(wide expressively)   (bebop)
narrow expressively   quartal
(riff-like)   other (specify)_____

••

General Comments:

Tenor Madness

5/22/65

43

44

46

48

Tenor Madness

Sonny Rollins

Tenor Madness - Melodic Patterns

ARTIST_____ **Sonny Rollins**_____   Page_____

Title of composition: **Newk's Fadeaway**

Album: **Sonny and the STARS**

Recording company: **Prestige 7269**

Date: **December 1951**

Leader or sideman: **Leader**

Instrument: **Tenor Saxophone**

••

Tune type (circle one or more):

    blues   (jazz original)
    ballad   (bebop)
    modal   Latin/Afro-Cuban/etc.
    standard   other (specify)_____
    free

Tempo: ♩=120

Key: **Concert B♭ (Tenor C)**

Dramatic devices (circle and describe):

    (vibrato)
    (slurs)
    rips
    growls
    (glissandi)
    (articulation) (specify): **bebop phrasing**
    alternate fingerings
    harmonics
    other (specify):

Tessitura: **middle to high**

Scale preferences (circle one or more):

    (major (and derivatives))   blues
    (whole tone)   (pentatonic)
    diminished   chromatic
    diminished whole tone   (other) (specify):
    lydian dominant   **seventh**_____

Prevailing scale patterns: **see attached sheets**

Recurrent patterns: (A) II V7   **see attached sheets**

                     Turnbacks

                     Cycles

            (B) Melodic patterns **see attached sheets**

            (C) Rhythmic patterns

            (D) Other formulae (I VI II V; III VI II V; half-step progressions, etc.)

••

PERFORMANCE PRACTICE

Developmental techniques: simple to complex
(circle and describe)   complex to simple   **maintains same level of intensity**

                 single climax
                 (many climaxes)

                 (vertical)
                 horizontal

                 (chord referential)
                 thematic referential

                 (use of sequence) call and response

                 use of quotes (what and where)

                 (use of substitutions) **half step sideslip**

                 rhythmic practices: double time
                                  half time
                                  assymetrical groupings
                                (reiterative)
                                non-reiterative
                 describe relationship to the basic time: **on top**

                 some use of $\overset{3}{\sqcap\!\!\!\flat\flat\flat}$ **to slow down the time**

                 melody: folk-like   (bluesy)
                       (wide expressively)   (bebop)
                       narrow expressively   quartal
                       riff-like   other (specify)_____

••

General Comments: **This solo contains most of the licks and patterns which
were Sonny's favorites during his early career.**

Newk's Fade-away

Sonny Rollins

55

Newk's Fade-away

Sonny Rollins

C Melodic Patterns

Newk's Fade-away   Melodic Patterns (cont.)

＊ = favorite melodic patterns

Notice how Sonny imposes the G seventh scale over the first 8 of "Rhythm" changes.

ARTIST_____ **Sonny Rollins** _____   Page_____

Title of composition: **Tune Up**

Album: **Newk's Time**

Recording company: **Blue Note 84001**

Date: **Sept. 1958**

Leader or sideman: **Leader**

Instrument: **Tenor Saxophone**

••

Tune type (circle one or more):   blues   (jazz original)
                                         ballad   (bebop)
                                         modal   Latin/Afro-Cuban/etc.
                                         standard   other (specify)_____
                                         free

Tempo: ♩=138

Key: **D (Tenor E)**

Dramatic devices (circle and describe):   (vibrato)
                                              (slurs)
                                              rips
                                              growls
                                              glissandi
                                              (articulation) (specify): **varied**

                                              alternate fingerings
                                              harmonics
                                              other (specify):

Tessitura: **entire range**

Scale preferences (circle one or more):   (major (and derivatives))   blues
                                            (whole tone)   pentatonic
                                            (diminished)   chromatic
                                            diminished whole tone   (other) (specify):
                                            (lydian dominant)   **seventh**

60

Prevailing scale patterns: **recurrent diminished scale patterns** (see attached sheets)

Recurrent patterns: (A) II V7 **see attached sheets**

Turnbacks

Cycles

(B) Melodic patterns **see attached sheets**

(C) Rhythmic patterns

(D) Other formulae (I VI II V; III VI II V; half-step progressions, etc.)

••

PERFORMANCE PRACTICE

Developmental techniques: (simple to complex)
(circle and describe) complex to simple

(single climax)
many climaxes

(vertical)
horizontal

(chord referential) **both**
(thematic referential)

(use of sequence) call and response

use of quotes (what and where)

use of substitutions

rhythmic practices: double time
half time
assymetrical groupings
(reiterative)
non-reiterative

describe relationship to the basic time: **on top**

melody: folk-like _____   bluesy
(wide expressively)   (bebop)
narrow expressively   quartal
(riff-like)   other (specify)_____

••

General Comments:

Tune Up

solo by Sonny Rollins

63

64

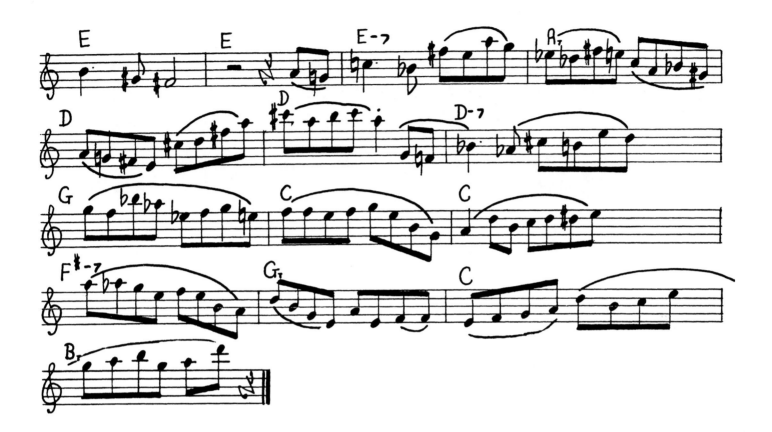

Tune Up

Sonny Rollins

Most of the melodic patterns are sequential and are found on the major chords. (see solo)

* favorite patterns

ARTIST_____**Sonny Rollins**_____   Page_____

Title of composition: **Airegin**

Album: **Bag's Groove**

Recording company: **Prestige 7109**

Date: **June 1954**

Leader or sideman: **Sideman**

Instrument: **Tenor Saxophone**

....

Tune type (circle one or more):

blues	(jazz original)
ballad	(bebop)
modal	Latin/Afro-Cuban/etc.
standard	other (specify)_____
free	

Tempo: ♩=120

Key: **F minor (Tenor G minor)**

Dramatic devices (circle and describe):

(vibrato)
(slurs)
rips
growls
glissandi
(articulation) (specify): **bebop phrasing**

alternate fingerings
harmonics
other (specify):

Tessitura: **entire range**

Scale preferences (circle one or more):

(major (and derivatives))	blues
whole tone	pentatonic
diminished	chromatic
diminished whole tone	(other) (specify):
lydian dominant	**seventh**

Prevailing scale patterns: **see attached sheet**

Recurrent patterns: (A) II V7   **see attached sheet**

              Turnbacks

              Cycles

       (B) Melodic patterns   **see attached sheet**

       (C) Rhythmic patterns

       (D) Other formulae (I VI II V; III VI II V; half-step progressions, etc.)

••

PERFORMANCE PRACTICE

Developmental techniques: simple to complex ⎫
   (circle and describe)   complex to simple ⎬ **maintains a constant level**
                       single climax   ⎬   **of excitement**
                       many climaxes   ⎭

                       (vertical)
                       horizontal

                       (chord referential) **but a few allusions to the theme**
                       thematic referential

                       (use of sequence) call and response

                       use of quotes (what and where)

                       use of substitutions

                       rhythmic practices: double time
                                    half time
                                    assymetrical groupings
                                  (reiterative)
                                  non-reiterative
                     describe relationship to the basic time: **on top**

                     melody: folk-like   bluesy
                          (wide expressively)   (bebop)
                        narrow expressively   quartal
                        riff-like   other (specify)_____

••

General Comments:

Airegin

solo by
Sonny Rollins

71

72

Airegin

Sonny Rollins

II V₇'s

74

MELODIC PATTERNS

ARTIST_____**Sonny Rollins**_____   Page_____

Title of composition: **Hold 'em Joe**

Album: **Sonny Rollins on Impulse**

Recording company: **Impulse A - 91 or AS - 91**

Date: **July 8, 1965**

Leader or sideman: **Leader**

Instrument: **Tenor Saxophone**

****

Tune type (circle one or more):

blues	jazz original
ballad	bebop
modal	(Latin/Afro-Cuban/etc.)
standard	(other)(specify)_____ **Calypso**_____
free	

Tempo: ♩ =126

Key: **Concert B♭ (Tenor C)**

Dramatic devices (circle and describe):

(vibrato)
slurs
rips
growls
(glissandi)
(articulation)(specify): **varied**

alternate fingerings
harmonics
(other)(specify): **embellishment**

Tessitura: **entire range**

Scale preferences (circle one or more):

(major (and derivatives))	blues
whole tone	pentatonic
diminished	(chromatic)
diminished whole tone	(other)(specify):
lydian dominant	_____**seventh**_____

Prevailing scale patterns:

Recurrent patterns: (A) II V7

     Turnbacks } not relevant because of the nature of the composition

     Cycles }

    (B) Melodic patterns   See entire solo from the standpoint of melodic shapes, sequential patterns, embellishing devices, etc.

    (C) Rhythmic patterns

    (D) Other formulae (I VI II V; III VI II V; half-step progressions, etc.)

....

PERFORMANCE PRACTICE

Developmental techniques: (simple to complex)
  (circle and describe)   (complex to simple)   both

     (single climax) on return
     many climaxes

     (vertical)
     (horizontal)   both

     (chord referential)
     (thematic referential)   both

     (use of sequence) call and response

     use of quotes (what and where)

     use of substitutions

    rhythmic practices: (double time)
      half time
      assymetrical groupings
      (reiterative)
      non-reiterative
   describe relationship to the basic time: **on top**

    melody: (folk-like)   bluesy
      (wide expressively)   bebop
      narrow expressively   quartal
      riff-like   other (specify)_____

....

General Comments:

Hold'em Joe

7/8/65

ARTIST_____**Sonny Rollins**_____   Page_____

Title of composition: **Keep Hold of Yourself**

Album: **Next Album**

Recording company: **Milestone MSP 9042**

Date: **July 1972**

Leader or sideman: **Leader**

Instrument: **Tenor Saxophone**

....

Tune type (circle one or more):

blues	(jazz original)
ballad	bebop
(modal)	Latin/Afro-Cuban/etc.
standard	other (specify)_____
free	

Tempo: ♩=124

Key: **C Minor (Tenor D minor)**

Dramatic devices (circle and describe):

(vibrato)
(slurs)
rips
growls
glissandi
(articulation) (specify): **varied**

alternate fingerings
harmonics
other (specify):

Tessitura: **medium**

Scale preferences (circle one or more):

major (and derivatives)	blues
whole tone	(pentatonic)
diminished	chromatic
diminished whole tone	(other) (specify):
lydian dominant	**seventh**

Prevailing scale patterns: **see attached sheets**

Recurrent patterns: (A) II V7   **see attached sheets**

                        Turnbacks

                        Cycles

          (B) Melodic patterns   **see attached sheets**

          (C) Rhythmic patterns

          (D) Other formulae (I VI II V; III VI II V; half-step progressions, etc.)

••

PERFORMANCE PRACTICE

Developmental techniques: simple to complex   **Maintains same level of intensity**
   (circle and describe)   complex to simple   **throughout.**

                        single climax
                        many climaxes   **same level**

                        vertical
                        (horizontal)

                        chord referential
                        (thematic referential)

                        (use of sequence) call and response

                        use of quotes (what and where)

                        use of substitutions

                        rhythmic practices: double time
                                        half time
                                        assymetrical groupings
                                      (reiterative)
                                      non-reiterative
                        describe relationship to the basic time: **on top**

                        melody: (folk-like)   (bluesy)
                                (wide expressively)   bebop
                                narrow expressively   quartal
                                (riff-like)   other (specify)_____

••

General Comments:

Keep Hold of Yourself

Tenor Sax Solo
Sonny Rollins

86

Keep Hold of Yourself

Sonny Rollins

Melodic Patterns

The Language

All of the II V7 and melodic patterns, cycles, turnarounds, etc., which have been abstracted from a wide variety of musical situations, have been transposed to the key of C. In order to derive maximum benefits from their study, the reader is encouraged to transpose the patterns to all keys, varying musical components such as tempo, meter, volume, register, vibrato and articulation.

Whenever possible, the author has grouped many of the melodic patterns according to scale or mode; e.g., lydian dominant patterns, diminished patterns, etc. This practice allows the student to see at a glance the soloist's scale preferences in a variety of musical environs. (The chord to scale syllabus in the front of this book will be an invaluable aid in determining why and how the soloist chose a particular scale).

Once the material has been understood and internalized, the reader should begin striving to personalize the myriad patterns and scales in a way compatible with his/her own musical philosophy.

Finally, this series of style studies provides the jazz musician/teacher at whatever level of development the unique opportunity to "study with" John Coltrane, Miles Davis, Charlie Parker, et al.

II V₇ Patterns

Sonny Rollins

94

The above has countless variants in the vocabulary

of Sonny Rollins.

has many variants.

Melodic Patterns

Sonny Rollins

✳ = favorite patterns

104

107

Whole Tone Patterns

Sonny Rollins

Blues Patterns

Diminished Patterns